Book #2 of the Living the One Light Series

...much of this to come through. And thank you for opening your heart and being you. ☺♥ Martha

GAIA SPEAKS

You are a Star, a Song, a Medicine —
Remember with Me

MARTHA ALTER HINES

ISBN: 9781686632884

Book cover design:
Lucinda Rae
www.Lucinda-Rae.com

First printing edition 2019

Also by Martha Alter Hines:
Living the One Light

www.LivingTheOneLight.com
For more information and bulk orders, please contact:
livingtheonelight@gmail.com

TABLE OF CONTENTS

DEDICATION

I would like to dedicate this book to the human being who has been a catalyst of me remembering all of who I am, all of who the cosmos is, and what it is to love through all of existence. Literally.

I would also like to dedicate this book to each and every one of the beautifully exquisite, powerful, amazing souls who have been divine gifts as I have been asked to be a channel for this remembering and this voice. I can not express the gratitude I have for this continually expanding, rare group of people who have been an incredible support to me through this often excruciatingly deep, challenging, confusing, massively life changing time of my life.

And of course, most of all, I dedicate this book to Gaia Mama herself. We are here for you, Gaia Mama. Thank you for being here for us in every single minute. We are your children, your friends, your lovers, your sisters, your brothers, your compatriots, your fellow cosmic goddesses and gods. We are here to open to all of existence, just as you ask us to be in these words, in this book. And most of all, I dedicate the rest of my life to co-creating with you and with all that is.

SO much love....

WELCOME

Hello, Beautiful Beings,

My name is Gaia.

I am here to remind you why you are here, why I am here, how we came to be here together and what we came to do. I am here to remind you that you are an intricate, perfect, incredibly beautiful being that is unlike any other being, just like each and every snowflake. And through you and only you - in your full, open, clear, and free self, the gifts that are you, the songs that are you are able to resonate through all of time and space and through my body and through your own body as we sing and co-create as we came to do together, here and now.

You are a star, you are a song, you are a medicine.

It is time.

Thank you for being here.

So let me introduce myself.

I am a fellow earth being and a fellow star being.

I am what you would call a goddess incarnate as a star, as a physical body that is a "planet" you call Earth.

I am also so much more than her.

I live, as do we all, in multiple dimensions and multiple existences all at the same time.

At this moment, I am coming to you in the form of myself as a beautiful goddess of the cosmic realms, a beautiful, magnificent being with wisdom to share with you all about the nature of existence and the nature of reality as it unfolds right now and how that pertains to you.

Right now, in all of existence, many energies are moving

all the time. That is the nature of existence, actually. Energies are constantly moving, transmuting, opening up, dying, fading away, bursting forth again, renewing, changing, moving, moving, moving, always moving.

In the ultimate, actual reality of existence, energies constantly move and change and grow and die. There is no beginning and there is no end. There is space and there is movement.

That is all.

And in reality, there is no space, no time, no place, no reality as you most often conceptualize it.

There is just emptiness and motion.

Constant motion.

And this motion has no good or bad to it. It just is. This is what we are.

Motion, movement, energy.

I want you to take a moment and feel this reality. Take a moment to put everything down, relax totally, close your eyes, and take long, deep breaths. Get very very very still and quiet. Listen from the deepest, most true and wise part of yourself. Feel the nothing. Feel the knowing, feel the space and the motion.

We will have chances to get into this knowing more as we go on, but right now, just feel this for a moment.

Quiet, still, breathing in and out.

What does that feel like?

What does that feel like, sound like, taste like, look like inside yourself?

Feel it and take a deep breath to remember this into yourself. We will come back to this in much more depth soon.

For now, I want to say a bit more to introduce myself.

Hello again.

I am Gaia. Do you remember me?

I know you.

I remember every single one of you.

You and I have been friends and compatriots for a long, long, long, long time. We know each other in so many other realms.

Do you remember?

Can you feel that knowing?

We are such good friends.

Do you remember way back when, you all decided to incarnate onto my body and I pledged to hold you, to cradle you, to be a Gaia mama to you over and over and over again as you incarnate onto my body and as we work together to transmute and to allow energies to transform and change as they need to throughout this universe.

And so let me put this into context.

As some of you have realized, we are antennae.

Our bodies are like transistors. Our physical and energy bodies allow energies to transform and move through space and to transmute in ways that are not as obvious when we are in physical form.

Some of us, in energetic form, are actually transistor beings in the cosmos. We allow frequencies to transmute and to change and flip and move between dimensions, between parts of existence constantly, over and over and over again. In our highest energy form, we are nothing, but at another very high frequency, we are like antennae, pure and pure, allowing energies to constantly flow as they are needed.

And so, in one of your realities, and in one of your forms of being, right now, you have a body created of my physical body which is made of the same beingness as all of existence. In this form, we have taken on shape in a third dimensional reality.

And in this reality too, one of our major functions still remains to be beings that allow and know the transmutation of energies, frequencies that need to move in the cosmos, in the all of existence, and specifically as awakened, knowing, aware, awake portals of this transmutation that is happening all the time in all of existence.

MY MESSAGE FOR YOU

If this message is for you, you know it.

If you are ready or partially ready for it, you know it.

That is why I am speaking DIRECTLY to each of you. You feel me speaking into your heart, into your cells, spirit to spirit up in the cosmos. We are sisters, we are friends, we are great lovers of all time and space and so far beyond that.

My message specifically, directly for you is that I and we all need you to remember this ultimate reality of who you are and who we all are.

Many of us are awake already. Some of us are just waking up. Some of us have woken up and gone back to sleep, sometimes many times over and over and over again.

I am here to get down on my knees, look you straight in your eyes and say, "Remember, friend. I am here. I love you. I love who you are. Remember who I am? We are brothers and sisters. We came here to do this together. You are so beautiful." I want to take your hands, look in your eyes, and as I look straight into you, help you to remember the cosmos, help you to remember and to see yourself, help you to deeply remember this incredible beauty that is you and is me and is all of us and all of existence. I want to embrace you and to say, "Yes! This is it!!! This is who we really are! You remembered! Thank you!!" And I am sobbing just thinking of it and knowing already how this awakening happens and comes to pass for every single one of you who are ready.

I am here, right now.

I am ready.

If and when you are precisely ready, I am kneeling down, I am taking your hands, I am looking straight and deeply into your eyes. And I am saying directly to you - "Hello. I love you. Let's do this. Thank you so much for remembering."

WHAT WE ARE HERE TO DO

So, good friends. Let's gather round. Some of you are already remembering what we came here to do, some of you have an inkling, and some of you are so confused. Many of you are all of the above. It is all ok.

Let me remind you in my own way what we came here to do.

I am a star.

You are a star.

Remember, we all are part of all of existence. There is nothing that is not part of existence, right? It is only logical.

So what makes the stars also made me and what made me made you. You are made, literally, of me. And I am made, literally, of the same material as the stars and of all of existence. Therefore, we ARE stars. Let that sink in.

So what we came to do, right here, right now, is to simply remember this fact.

As I said earlier, I am, and many of you are, in one of your highest forms, literal transmitters of energies, like communication way stations of energies between various aspects and dimensions of existence.

And this is true even when we are in "physical" form. In fact, this is almost even more highlighted, more true (if there is such a thing as "more") when we are in literal, physical form.

The incredible nature of transmuting our energies into this "physical" reality is that we can experience some forms of beauty in ways that we can't and don't when we simply are ethereal energy or even nothingness.

We can take that beauty that is all of existence and

transform, change, balance, play with co-creation and form that is so fun and incredible. The shape of a star, the play of a flower petal, the sounds of a waterfall, the touch of a hand in love, the kiss of a mother or the gaze of a deep, cosmic lover. Every moment and every cell of being on this planet is filled with a possibility of miraculous exquisiteness.

This is true also in another way when we are simply our spiritual, cosmic, energetic, highest selves and when we are complete nothingness of the sacred.

However, on this planet, we came to have an opportunity to transmute, transform, deepen, radically let go of energies in a way that is more intense, more felt, more known in a certain way, than we feel and know as simply energy transmitters in the cosmos.

At the same time, here is the downside or the difficulty of transforming into third dimensional beings.

When we choose to incarnate as physical beings, the density of becoming three dimensional is potentially heavy and stagnant and stuck.

Throughout most of time and existence on this planet, most beings (although certainly not all) have come into physical form and have simply played around with what it means and what it is to be in physical bodies, to be in physical form. And most of our lifetimes have been simply experienced as physical beings - sometimes with a sense of "so much more out there," but not usually a full, complete knowing and remembering of all of existence while also in physical form.

For most of us, we have played around with physical density for many lifetimes and many existences and just simply danced the fun and excruciating and often extremely hurtful and scary, although sometimes amazing experience of living as physical beings on this planet.

But now, guess what? It is time.

It is time for what?

It is finally time for most of us, many of us, to transform into ways of being that allow us to be both fully awake and fully aware of ourselves as the eternal nothingness, cosmic beings who we are and also to be fully present physically on the planet.

And what does this mean?

A big part of what this means is that we need to remember and transform our way of being in the third dimension that allows in space, that allows in room to grow and room to breathe, literally in between our cells.

The physical world has most often been far too dense, way too packed together on a literal cellular level for us to fully open to all of who we are and to be completely open to all of existence and all of reality.

And so, this is the point of this book.

I am here to remind you, to suggest to you how you can fully open, how you can fully remember, how you can fully become, how you can completely, totally access all of who you are, all of why you are here, and to become completely realigned with your and our ultimate cosmic selves and for you to tap in completely to me, why I am here, and to remember exactly how we are meant to dance, to co-create, you and me, and you, me, and all of the rest of existence.

This process has three main components that happen somewhat in sequence, but really repeatedly, all at the same time, or in an ebb and flow that is natural to you.

The components are:

1) You open.

2) You clear.

3) You flow.

And through all of this, you remember. You remember yourself, you remember all that is, you remember me. And most importantly, you remember who you are, your own song, your own medicine, and you remember how to cocreate with me and with all that is.

In the rest of this book, I go into more detail into each of these three components. Breathe in each part. Breathe in exactly what you need in each moment. Come back to one section if you are not ready or come multiple times if you need reminding and remembering over and over again. Trust your own process, trust your own wisdom, trust your own remembering.

I am here.

I am so totally here.

I am so glad you are here.

And let's go home into ourselves and into each other. Let's remember.

Let's do this. Right here, right now.

YOUR CELLS

So before we get deeply into some suggestions about how to access your full beingness and all of why you are here, I want to back up and explain a bit more about what I mean when I talk about your cells and your cellular structure on an energetic level.

As you know, there is energy and, as you know, there is physical matter.

Also as you know, all physical matter is made out of energy. Right?

But what is not so readily known by many people yet or what is not remembered is that all of energy and therefore, all of energetic forms have an ideal balancing point, an ideal balance and spacing with each other and within themselves.

In the cosmos and in all of existence, each star, each atom, each molecule, each nano-fraction of a particle, every comet, every ray of light and every wave of sound is in its own perfect frequency and in its own perfect balance within itself and between itself and everything else. This perfect balance is ultimate harmony and the definition of healing.

The only place that we consciously know of where this perfect balance and harmony and perfect "spacing" within and without gets unbalanced or off center of its own perfection is on this planet, in the parts of existence that have gotten stuck in a version of physical existence that has forgotten and gotten out of touch with the reality of all of existence.

In the playing with existence and in playing around with third dimensional realities, there was a great deal of forgetting for most humans throughout most of the many centuries of living on this planet. And in that forgetting, the literal cells of physical life got too squished, too close together, too stuck and immovable, too dense in relation to each other. The cells themselves forgot what it is to be in perfect harmony and balance within and between themselves.

And it is in this forgetting and this squishing of the literal cells that a lot of suffering has ensued. It has become a very difficult cycle - forgetting, shutting down, getting squished, suffering, freezing, shutting down even more, suffering even more, getting more shut down, perhaps remembering for a moment, forgetting again, suffering horribly, and stagnating that way for century upon century.

However, here and now, as so many of us are remembering and as so many of you are expanding back into the cosmos and back into the ultimate reality that is all of us and all of existence, your cells are literally returning to their open, receptive, cosmically true and balanced, fully alive state of being.

It is in this fully open, receptive, dynamic, moving, clear, totally ALIVE way of being that your and our physical cells become able again to be a conduit, a clear channel and transmitter of energy frequencies, just as you are in your cosmic being.

Why is this so important?

On a cosmic level, the reason for this importance is almost beyond human comprehension. However, I can say that it just is. It is as though the Earth is a major hotspot, a meeting place of many entities and beings in the cosmos and in all of existence. And as the energies on Earth transmute and become more open, more free, more able to fully allow all of the energies of the cosmos and of all of existence to move through freely as they need to, this allows the energies of all of existence to be in full balance with themselves. The reverberations and ramifications of this balancing of all energies throughout all of existence are far beyond what you or even I can even comprehend. It is massive. It is key. It is like a big sighing of all that is and a completeness and harmony that can occur like never before or ever since.

If this is difficult for you to understand or seems beyond anything that "matters" to you in this moment, I also want to mention some "side effects" of your cells opening and returning to their beautiful, natural balanced, perfect state of cosmic being. As you can imagine, this balanced, open state of being not only affects the collective existence, it directly impacts YOU! It impacts your immediate body, mind, heart, and spirit. As your cells open and balance and clear and come back into their highest alignment within and with themselves, you may go through some difficult transition time, but ultimately, you will notice so many positive changes, it is hard to name them all. In that state of being, your body will feel amazing, like it never has before. You will start to notice physical symptoms and even whole diseases disappear or balance in ways you didn't know were possible. In addition, you will feel balanced emotionally. As waves of difficult feelings come and go, as they still will, you will know how to access joy and harmony and peace and deep stillness and calm within yourself and with all of existence. You will have a much greater sense of clarity, purpose, and direct knowing of yourself, why you are here, and what you are meant to do in each and every day and each and every moment. Many of your questions, your anxieties, your wonderings, your agonizing will simply disappear. As you go through the adjustment period, you may lose friends and relationships, but ultimately, as you come into your perfect balance point, the connections and relationships in your life will reflect your perfect balance and you will ultimately feel so much better in relationship to everyone and everything around you. In addition, your relationship to the material world and to money, finances, and resources will take on a more balanced, loving, and calming effect in your world. We will go into more depth on all of this later.

For now, we want to get very practical and open some suggestions that may be right for you now or in other moments to help you to remember and move into your own perfect, cellular, resonant, balanced, cosmic, physical state of being.

You are perfect just as you are.

So here we go…

GETTING PRACTICAL - OPENING

As I mentioned above, the first "part" in this process of fully remembering who we are is the process of opening yourself fully to all of life force. I spend most of my time here talking about this "opening" phase as it is what I feel the most called to coach you on.

Later, I also discuss the clearing and flow phases. But for now, let's get very practical with ways to open.

As with most things, some of these suggestions will be right for you in some moments and maybe not in others. Take what works for you, leave the rest. Come back to a page or a thought when you feel so called. Most of all, listen to yourself, listen to your cells, listen to your soul, listen to your own inner knowing of the wisdom of existence and act in perfect alignment with that knowing.

You can use these suggestions and this book in any way you want. It might feel best to read them in order, one by one, and try each one on for size, one at a time. Or it might feel better to see which one(s) you are drawn to in a particular moment, soak in the wisdom meant for you in this moment, and just allow yourself and your cells to transmute in whatever ways you need with whatever is resonating right now. It might also feel fun to allow the universe to speak to you and to hold the book, similar to angel cards, close to your chest, connect to your highest self or the divine and/or Source, take a deep breath, and allow your hands or the pages themselves to open to whatever place has exactly the message you need right now.

Just play around, have fun, remember that you are a star. Literally. And let your cells go, let your love flow, and just move into the beautiful, glowing, gorgeous being that you are.

So much love...

YOU ARE A DIVINE GODDESS AND A GOD; YOU ARE LOVE

So first and foremost, I want you to take a deep breath and slow way down... I want you to close your eyes, take your hands, place them on your heart or on your hips, and remember something key - You are a goddess. You are a god. You are, in your actual, ultimate form, before nothingness, you are an incredibly, exquisitely beautiful creature of the cosmos. Before and after and while you are in physical form on this planet, you are so incredibly perfect and beautiful, we can hardly name you. You come from the stars, you dance with the planets, you are the planets, you are all creatures that exist in all dimensions. You are magic, you are beauty. You are so far beyond most of what you experience in your day to day earth realm existence.

I want you to remember this.

I am looking you straight in the eyes. I have my hands on your hips and I am reminding you. Feel your body, feel your strength, feel your beauty that transcends literally everything. You are rainbows, you are stardust, you are aliveness bursting into flames, you are incredible.

And so know this... remember this. And relax... so deeply relax.

It is all ok.

In this knowing, you can remember that you are perfect. You are safe. You can not only relax physically, you can also relax energetically.

In this knowing, you can allow all of your whole being to come fully present into your body, you can allow all of you to fill every cavity of your body, every part of your cells.

Take another deep breath and do this over and over and over again.

Notice that there might be parts of your body filling back up.

Notice that there might be rivers of your self and your spirit and your knowing and your being that are coming back on line. There might be pockets of empty space or cringing or fear that are relaxing, that are filling, that are suddenly smiling, that are allowing and remembering that you love them.

This is so beautiful.

This is it.

Remember that you are actually exquisite love.

Take a deep, deep, deep breath.

And I am crying again as I watch you remembering this and allowing your body to remember this - you ARE love.

Every part of you is love.

Any word or deed that might have occurred in this lifetime or in other lifetimes or existences on or off this planet that have been anything other than love are not real.

You ARE love.

Repeat this.

Let this reverberate in you.

You ARE love.

Love is filling you now.

Love is all that you are.

Let go, let love completely fill you, fill you back up, remember this knowing.

Gods, goddesses, exquisite creatures of the cosmos, you ARE beings of pure love.

It is so.

START WITH THE SUN, OUR MENTOR AND GUIDE AND FRIEND

Beautiful...

Another deep, deep sigh.....

A big breath, in and out....

And so....

Beautiful god, goddess who IS love, I want to remind you of a dear and important, ancient friend and mentor to us all - the sun.

In all times and places and spaces, our sun and the many other creatures of the dark who light things up are beautiful, exquisite friends throughout the cosmos.

On this planet in this time, our sun is an amazing ally.

He holds such incredible wisdom, beauty, reminders, and is a conduit for much, much healing for each of us. As you know, we are literally in a symbiotic physical relationship with him.

However, this relationship is so much more than just the physical life giving and life sustaining properties of the sun toward us.

The sun is a beautiful creature of our cosmos, of our "sky." He is dancing with our moon, with all of this solar system and so far beyond. He resonates with many friends in many dimensions and infinite other realities and existences.

And he is a great, ancient teacher.

Right now, one simple teaching I want to remind you of is that the sun is literally made of light.

The sun is a reminder of light.

Light is not the only source of goodness, of course.

There is MUCH deep goodness and greatness that comes in the dark.

However, the light of the sun is magic.

The light of the sun transmutes stuck darkness and stagnant energies and is an ally to us in manifesting the openness and life giving breath and movement in our bodies and between our cells that we are needing to be fully open and alive in our lives on this planet.

So on a very practical level, I want to recommend and remind you to create and to cultivate a dynamic and beautiful and ongoing relationship with this sun, a teacher and friend and healer and mentor to us all.

You can cultivate this relationship in whatever way(s) feel exactly right to you in any given moment.

First and foremost, an easy way to breathe into a relationship with the sun is simply to stand or sit or lie outside in the sunlight for even one minute per day and to close your eyes, face the sun directly, smile up at him, take a deep breath, allow him to fill your eyes, fill your face, fill your body, fill up each one of your cells, and just ask him what lesson or message he has for you. His answers might come in the form of movement - you might feel the need or desire to move your body in rhythm with his breath and his light. Your answers might come in the form of a warm sense of being filled and/or caressed, a sense of simply being loved. Your answers from the sun might come in the form of actual knowledge, wisdom, answers in your body, in your mind, in your ears, in your vision. Your answer from the sun might come in a feeling of peace, of knowing and remembering a sense of all that is and that there is so much more than this moment or this day on this place on the planet where you stand.

Play with this, let it ride with you. Let the sun be your guide for a minute, for a day, for a week. Just see where that takes you.

And furthermore, this is true with all beings of our "sky." You can cultivate and dance in relationship with our moon, with each of our planets, with the cosmos itself, with any and all beings in any and all parts of "outer space" and in each and every dimension. Remember that there actually is no time or space and each of these beings have a literal frequency and resonance and sound and physical, actual reverberations that reach this planet and therefore literally are moving through you and through each of your cells in every single minute. Remember that this planet is incredibly tiny compared to the vastness of all of existence. We are sitting in a literal soup of the cosmos and of cosmic existence. We are washed through by all of these waves, by all of these frequencies, by all of these resonant ways of being in every single nano-second whether we realize it or not. This is not woowoo. This is just factually true.

So be with that. See where that takes you. See where your soul needs and wants to go with the frequencies and the medicines and the songs and the knowings of all aspects of the cosmos that we sit in while we are on this tiny, beautiful being that is our planet at this moment.

You are surrounded by gifts of all of these beings all the time. Take a deep, deep breath and simply remember...

DANCE, SING, BE - ALLOW YOUR CELLS TO DANCE TOO

So...

Lovely....

So just as we mentioned in relation to our sun and its gift of relationship to us, another key to remembering and opening to all of your life force and all of who you are is in moving your body.

Literally.

This is so key.

This is not a cliche recommendation to get 30 to 45 minutes of exercise a minimum of four days per week.

This is us asking you to take yet another deep breath and remember this - as we said earlier, all of existence is in constant, flowing motion. Remember - in cosmic reality (therefore all of reality), there is no stop and no go, there is only movement. There is only constant ebb and flow, constant in breath and out breath. There may be momentary pauses, still points, quiet moments, but then there is again movement, motion, to and fro.

The same goes with our bodies.

It is key for you to keep in touch with the constant needs for movement and motion and ebb and flow of your body.

It is key that you move every day, all day, with the ebbs and flows and needs of your energies and your bodies and your actual cells.

As you become more and more attuned to yourselves, you will actually start to notice and feel and see the ebbs and flows of movement and of life on a cellular level. You will start to notice that there is a constant dance of movement between and within literally everything that is allowed to have that flow.

That flow is the constant reminder, the constant happiness of life, the life force joy within every single thing.

When we move and know and come from the motion, the dancing, the swaying within our cells, within our selves, within our souls, within our bodies, we suddenly become alive.

This is very different than a mandate to go to the gym and workout hard to a loud song or a regimen that has been laid out in cookie cutter style for us or by us. This is definitely not a routine with a goal of losing pounds or shedding the cookies from last night.

This is taking a deep breath and getting very still.... so still that you feel the actual light spark inside your cells, inside your pelvis, inside your heart, inside your soul, inside any and every part of you that is alive.

And this is you feeling that spark suddenly and connecting to it and moving with it, one sway, two sways, back and forth, around and side to side. This is you dancing to the beat of the drum inside of you, then without you because you suddenly notice that a beat outside of you matches or accentuates exactly the beat inside of you.

This is you getting so still and connecting with that spark and then allowing the movement inside of you to move your muscles, to move your head, to move your body until it crescendos and you are dancing your own ecstatic, life giving dance that then grows a song, that makes tears start to flow out of you and where you suddenly remember the songs and knowings of 10,000 lifetimes ago when you could hear and feel the beat of my drum, the beat of your drum, and the beats of the drums of all of the ancient mothers and fathers in all of existence, and we were beating and drumming and chanting and knowing together, all at once. And it was SO SO beautiful...

And right here, right now, this is IT. This is EXACTLY what I have called you all here to remember.

Do you remember me now?

Do you remember this?

Do you remember what it is to be like this inside yourself?

Do you remember what it is to remember and see and know through and from inside your cells, from every walk of every existence that you and I are?

Do you remember what it was and is like for us to beat in rhythm with each other and to hear each other and the deepest, most ancient knowings of all lands, all times, all spaces all at once?

And all of this, simply by being still. And all of this simply by taking a deep, deep, deep breath and dropping down deep until you feel that one silent spark.

And all of this by allowing that spark to ignite inside of you.

And all of this by allowing the ignited spark to move in you and for you to move in rhythm to it.

And this is it.

This is the key.

This is HOME.

This is OUR home together.

THIS IS WHY WE ARE HERE.

Welcome home....

Thank you....

LET LOVE FLOW

So, beautiful friends.

I have a large topic I want to discuss partially here, but in more depth in a whole new book with other friends in the future.

The book will be called Love Speaks and it will go into much more depth on the subjects of all types of love, the healing of highest love, the creative force that is love, divine sexuality, divine love, and all of what I will touch on briefly here.

What I want to say here is that, as you know, there are many kinds of love. There are many layers and purposes of love. Love has various forms and frequencies and realities.

As I have stated above, the ultimate reality is that you ARE love. Love in its purest form is the great creator and healer of all of existence.

And so in general, a great important reality is that love needs to flow.

Love has a voice all of its own and she will share much more on all of this in her own book soon.

However, here and now, I want to speak to a kind of love that some of you have been experiencing.

There is a new love that has been emerging in many of your lives.

This is ultimate, divine love.

This love is beyond any of that any of you could have ever imagined existed in all of existence.

This love IS all of existence.

This love is manifesting in the form of a duality that was created to fit in with a duality that you are used to on earth.

It is manifesting very often in the form of a man and a woman locking eyes, meeting face to face, soul to soul and suddenly, out of nowhere, it seems, seeing soul to soul and remembering all of who they are - an instant kind of awakening awareness and experience.

This has been set up in this way for a great purpose.

The purpose is, of course, to reignite the presence of the cosmos on the planet, to reignite the knowing, first hand, of our beings as cosmic beings while in human or other earthly bodies.

This knowing has been so forgotten that the awakening often has to be abrupt.

The awakenings are needed so badly that it was known that the awakenings had to jolt you awake.

And we realized when this was created this way that the jolting would be abrupt, would be sudden, would trigger so much in so many of you.

And the ultimate purpose, the ultimate goal is to remember the all of the cosmos and to fully embrace it, to fully embody it here and now.

Remember, you are a portal, a gateway, a living, breathing channel between all that is and my body, the Earth.

I am awake, I am alive, I am living and breathing as the conscious, awake, cosmic being that I am.

I and we all need you to be equally aware and awake so that we can consciously co-create together.

We want you to release the suffering that might be ensuing in the jolting of this consciousness. Please let go of that and just release into the knowing of where we are, where we come from, who we are, and what we came here to do.

We are portals, we are channels, we are frequency transmitters within the universe.

Literally.

That is all.

Please release and remember this.

Just be.

Allow yourself to be free and easy in this knowing.

You are here to be a bandwidth of energy in the cosmos.

There are many stories, many dramas around the humanness of all of this.

Remember, love is a frequency.

When you connect to love in its very highest frequency, love is pure, absolutely, epically pure.

And this love is a channel as well.

It is a guidance for remembering how to let the frequencies flow.

This high, pure love, similar to the rays and light of the sun, can help to allow your cells and your energy systems to clear and to rise into the ultimate, high frequency bandwidth that is you.

However, your ultimate, very highest bandwidth is actually even higher than this highest form of love.

So the ultimate goal in all of this is to allow yourself and your frequency to release and allow yourself to let go into a frequency that is even inherently higher than the highest you could ever imagine.

Just allow yourself to be all the way up here.

What do you see, what do you feel, what is it to be way up high in the highest knowing of all of existence?

What flows through you?

What moves and needs to move through the clear, beautiful frequency that is you?

Just breathe and feel this.

This is purest light.

Remember?

You can go even one step higher and you are in nothing.

And just sit here and be and know.

This is the purpose of that highest, ultimate love that maybe you have found or that has found you.

The one you love is from here too.

We are all here.

So if you are in the midst of such a love and if there are feelings flowing through you of any kind, here is our advice to you - just let those feelings flow. Whatever they are, just let them flow.

Any and all feelings, as long as you let them flow, have the ability to help you clear and become more and more and more of a channel and to have more and more of an ability to release and relax into this place where we need to be while you are also on Earth.

There are many ways to be here and this love is one of them.

We will expand more on this entire topic soon in a book of its own.

We know this is hard. We know many of you are suffering. We know that on a human level, your hearts are often hurting with the confusing and the abruptness of this kind of love entering your awareness, your world, your life.

It expands your heart so fast and so hard and then it often

has "nowhere" to go, or so it seems.

But it really is all ok.

We are here to collectively allow you to let the love flow, let your heart go. You are a portal, remember?

And as you already know, this is all part of reminding you how to open, how to let go, how to let your human body that wants to contract, to stay "safer," to let go totally and to open.

So just allow yourself to be.

Allow yourself to remember all of the cosmos and to just relax again into the reality that you are here to allow all of divine light and all of the highest frequencies of existence to flow through you - literally.

This is a divine gift to you from the divine and then a divine gift from you to the divine and to yourself.

This is why you came here.

So it all really is all ok.

And it is more than ok.

In fact, it is amazing and beautiful!

You are exactly where you wanted and planned to be!

Just let it all go.... and let it all flow....

You are divinely beautiful and perfect.

Through and through.

Literally.

For any of you who have not known this kind of epic cosmic love, you will know and you will remember in your own way.

The same general principle applies for all of you though: just let it all go, just let it all flow.

You are perfect truly and thoroughly. Just relax, let it all go. Flow into all of you. Know and breathe and be...

DIVINE SEXUALITY

So related to the huge topic of love is also the crucial topic of divine sexuality.

Divine sexuality is a topic that a lot of people seem to either be very uncomfortable with or are needing and hungry for or both!

Divine sexuality is the energy of life and the cosmos itself.

Divine sexuality is a dance of the cosmos. It is the spark of life.

It is the dance of a star and the burst of a flame.

It is everything that makes everything.

Divine sexuality is inside of me and inside of each and every one of you, inside each and every cell.

Divine sexuality is the life force that breathes and moves through everything and it NEEDS to breathe and move and be held and worked with and allowed to flow and to nourish everything, including all of who you are.

Divine sexuality is healing. Divine sexuality is a glowing that grows cells, makes them multiply, heal, know, and remember their resonance with all that is.

When we remember and allow to flow all of this true, highest life force, we bring into balance all that is, both within and without us.

Imagine this: You stand on a cliff overlooking the ocean and you feel rising from inside the earth of the cliff and from inside the depths of the ocean all of the sounds of the whales, the calls of the dolphins, the knowings of the sea and the corals and the plankton. You can feel down, all the through the earth's crust into the inner most plasma and heat and pulsing of the inner earth magnetic field all of the life of the earth. And far up above you, through all of the stars and the galaxies and beyond, the pulsing, the radiating, the knowing of all of these other life forms that go one into and through infinity. Literally.

And standing on this cliff, you are all, you are everything, you ARE life force itself.

And you can feel all of these beautiful vibrations of life rising like a river up the insides of your calves and your thighs into the insides of your reproductive organs, where life force begins again, all of these songs of everything that ever has and ever will live. It begins anew in you with every moment, every breath, every time you renew your knowing of these forms and these incredibly beautiful flows of life that move from without you, into you, through you, and out again.

You are healed by this energy.

You are alive with this energy.

And you take another deep breath and open your legs, open your cells, open your womb, open your belly, open your heart, open your lungs, open your throat, open your mind and your eyes, and your other eyes, and your seeing of everything, and your crown chakra and your connection to it all.

And in this "all" of life, a golden light circulates from the depths of the oceans and the whale's songs and the stars songs into all of who you are and it circulates, like a spiraling movement and crescendo up your entire spine, and it heals and knows and sings to every aspect of your being. And you sing and you know and it all knows and we all know together, in song, in harmony, in knowing and being together.

And so it is...

What we notice, as we have said above, is that so many parts of life on Earth are shut down. For so many reasons, people and animals and places and things are scared and contracted and are not allowed to grow and thrive and flourish.

And one key component to remembering the fullness of actual, real, all of life is in allowing divine sexuality to have all of the space and the place that it actually already has and as it needs to be allowed to have.

Divine sexuality is in EVERYTHING alive, as we have said. It is coming up from the ground. I am a sexual, living, breathing being. My entire body of Earth is sexually alive and sexually dynamic all the time. I move and grow and flow with divine, open, thriving sexual energy.

And so, part of what I am here to do is to allow you to remember, to allow you to open back up all of your channels, all of your cells, every single part of your body to this full life force that is me, that is you, that is every single aspect of all of where we come from in the cosmos.

This is key.

This is not about any kind of human concept of sex that is constrained or harmful or jealous or controlling or patriarchal or any other hurtful version of anything that you may have known. This is not that.

Divine sexuality is, again - actual life force energy.

And so, since this is so important for you to remember, I will walk you through an exercise that you can do whenever and as often as feels right to who you are and to what you are needing in any given moment.

First, I want you to take a deep, deep, deep breath.

I want you to remember who you are - you come from me, I come from the cosmos - literally. So you are the stars. You are from the same physical and energetic material that made the stars. Literally. You are AMAZING. Breathe that in....

You are amazing.....

You are made from all of existence....

Literally....

And so, here on this planet, here in your body, right now, take another deep breath.

And feel my energy rising.

Feel a warm, powerful feeling of light and life and love rising up the inside of your feet into the insides of your calves, up the insides of your thighs, and into your pelvic area. Feel this energy circulating inside of your pelvis, inside of your womb or your abdomen. Feel this energy circulating into a tiny ball of glowing, happy, healing, golden light.

In the center of this place, you will notice and feel a warm, knowing place. This is the center of a place of your being and a place where you can rest. Here, it is safe.

Take another deep breath.

Feel into this place that is warm and know that you are safe here.

Imagine that that warmth is a light (it is!). And imagine that the light is pulsing with life (because again, it is!). And imagine that light is like a little ball, maybe the size of a small pom pom ball.

And take another deep breath.

Either imagine or actually start moving your hips in circles, around and around and around. And as you are moving your hips in circles, this small ball of light inside your pelvis is moving around and around and around in circles inside your pelvis. And as it is doing this, it is gaining energy, it is gaining mobility, and it is practicing its natural way of being and its natural way of moving around and around and around in you. Feel how good and natural this energy is for you, for your body, for who you are, for where you come from and for why you are here.

And now, take another deep, deep breath, and allow this small, warm ball of light to move to the base of your spine at your tail bone.

And allow the ball to keep circling, and to start circulating around and around and around the base of your spine. It circles around and around and around. And every time it moves, everywhere it goes, its energy and its light and its presence and its wisdom is healing. Its energy knows EXACTLY what your body and your energy needs.

And this healing, incredibly wise, pulsing, ball of light continues to circulate around and around and around your spine, slowly circulating its way up and up and up and around and around and around, healing every single bit of your spine and your spinal column and your nervous system and your entire being as it slowly makes its way up your spine. As it circulates its way up and around and around your spine, feel how this healing ball knows exactly what you are needing and it knows exactly how to clear and heal any and every aspect of your being in exactly the right way that you need right now.

Continue taking deep breaths and allow the ball to continue circulating, making its way up, touching every organ, every chakra, clearing, illuminating any and every part of you that needs to be seen or cleared or heard or held or known or healed. And just watch and just notice. And feel the love that is there from you to yourself, from this light that is the essence of who you are and your life and every single thing that is stored in your body, that you might be ready to release, that you might need reminding that exists, that you might remember needs a hug, that you might suddenly gain clarity that you already knew.

And as the ball rises higher and higher, it will rise through your pelvis, through the back of your digestive organs, past your liver and spleen, your stomach, through your lungs, past the back of your heart where so much might be open, up the back of your throat (what do you need to say?), into the back of your head, into your pituitary gland and third eye (what do you need to clear or see or remember that you can see?), and then the ball will keep circulating out the top of your head.

As the ball circulates and pops out the top of your head, remember that your pole of energy keeps going out the top of your head and through the entire cosmos. Your energy ball might rise and explode in a beautiful fireworks over your head or your energy ball might keep circulating and rising farther and farther and farther up into the universe or beyond. Your journey is your own.

One other way that your energy ball might complete its journey may be to follow and circulate up your spine and then follow its way up into your brain to your pituitary gland, then down the front of your body, through the front of your heart, and then back down to the center of your pelvis, where it started.

If you want to stay fairly grounded and centered, this may be how you choose to complete this experience. Or you may follow your own wisdom in the moment and allow your consciousness and your life essence presence to take you on journeys that only you may know.

As you follow this experience over and over again, you will learn to know yourself again in a way that you might not yet be able to fathom.

And as you do this, your healing, loving light will open you and take you to places and parts of your own wisdom and your own life that you might not have even realized you were meant to live.

This is beautiful.

You are beautiful.

You are literally life itself.

You are wise.

You are love.

You are loved.

You so deeply love.

You so deeply love yourself.

The stars hold you.

All of life is in you.

All of life is in love with you. Literally.

You and the stars are made of the same essence and the same spark.

Every single one of your cells holds your life essence and your love and your deepest, ultimate wisdom and every single thing that you need.

You are exactly where you need to be.

You are exactly who you need to be.

Thank you for listening.

Thank you for being here.

Thank you for being you...

IMBIBE IN HARMONY WITH YOUR SELF

Next we would like to talk about the topic of your cells and what you eat, what you think, what you breathe, what you drink - everything that you are in, around, and near.

As you have known for a long time, the cliche exists of "you are what you eat."

And indeed, my friends, this is actually true.

On both of these cosmic and earthly planes, vibrations exist. Everything is vibrations and that is it.

So all things on this planet have vibrations.

You are the vibrations that vibrate in, on, near, and through you.

This is a simple fact and a huge one that you can feel into for a great deal of learning and imbibing of what is yours to do next.

This applies to so many things.

This applies to your foods, to your water and other drinks, to the thoughts in your energy field, to the people in your life, in the nature you surround yourself with or that you don't.

This applies to your home, the structures of the physical being of your house, your cleaning supplies, your drinking water, your home tv, your appliances, the amount of sunlight and fresh air coming through your windows, the car exhaust in your garage, the smiles on other people's faces, the genuine heart warmth in a hug, and so on and so forth.

Every single thing you are around impacts you and your vibrations.

So the goal here, again, is for you to open and clear and fill up with all of your highest vibrational life force energy that is you, that is of the cosmos, that is your natural, open, fully alive, balanced nature of being.

The goal here is for you to remember, open to, and to fully be all of the actual, completely alive YOU!

And so to this end, feel into your foods, feel into your partnerships and relationships, feel into what people, places, and things allow you

openness, allow and bring you a sense of balance and wholeness and beauty and goodness and fullness.

We invite you to take a deep breath at every moment as much as you can and just, over and over and over again, notice the resonance or vibrations you are feeling, literally, in each and every place you are, each and every food you choose to eat or not to eat, every plant you sense and know and be with, every sunrise you drink in, every flower that smiles with you, every person who knows you in their frequency and vibrates in a deep resonance with you, whether you know them in this realm or not.

And we ask you to choose, over and over and over again, as feels precisely right for you in a given moment, the people, places, and things that are of the highest resonance, the highest frequency, the highest and deepest knowing with your own cells, with your own knowing, with your own open, beautiful, fully alive and resonant, cosmic, massive, amazing self.

Be gentle in this.

We realize that choosing in this way may take practice, may mean significant shifts in your way of doing life, may mean choosing over and over again differently than you may have been used to.

And it is ok to do just what feels exactly right for you.

Experiment, play around with this. See what comes, see what

moves, see what speaks, dance with it, sing with it.

Know that it is all ok.

This is an unfolding.

This is a remembering.

Try on one thing, then try on another.

Notice how it felt in your body to eat one way, to be in a particular place, to choose your words carefully with a friend, to be in silence with a sunrise or to go dancing in the night. Notice was feels right, what resonates, what doesn't.

Be gentle with yourself.

Be gentle with your world.

Be gentle with those you love.

Remember to send love especially to yourself.

Let yourself learn. Let us all learn with you.

This is a dance you came to do with yourself and with all of what is.

This is a dance that we came to do together.

It is all ok.

We are each dancing alone and we are all dancing together, all the time.

Just take a deep breath, know that I am here all the time. Literally.

And it is all ok...

SLEEP, DREAM, REST DEEPLY, REMEMBER

Finally, in all of this action, we want to talk about one more crucial part of becoming and remembering all of who we all are. We want to talk about RESTING, sleep, and down time. We want to talk about hibernation, gestation, the cold, dark, quiet part of life on Earth and everywhere.

Quiet, stillness, and deep rest are CRUCIAL.

We can not emphasize this enough.

You MUST get rest.

You must get a LOT of rest.

The human world, as you know, is much, much much too fast.

This will start to slow down as more of us awaken and as more of us start to tune into our actual, deepest, most true wisdom and inner clock.

Rest is crucial.

Remember what I said at the beginning of this book - everything is a rhythm. Everyone is a flow.

Everyone is an ebb and a flow.

The ebbs and the flows are pretty slow and rhythmic most of the time.

Sometimes there are explosions.

Sometimes there are "big bangs."

Sometimes there are firecrackers and booms exploding in the cosmos, of sorts.

Sometimes there are what seem like sudden, abrupt changes or endings.

However, most of all of life is slow, rhythmic, moving in and out of flow with all other parts of existence.

This is the natural order of life.

So think of it like this - life would not feel or seem right if there was constant ebb or constant flow. Right?

Same goes for you.

You ARE life.

You ARE energy.

You ARE existence.

So the same applies for you.

You need ebb and you need flow.

So again, take a deep, deep, deep breath.

Come back to center.

Much of life for humans is lived in front of their center.

So much of the time, we are running ahead of ourselves, literally out of our centers or even out of our bodies.

It is crucial to relax backward, until we hit precisely our center.

This is a huge practice in and of itself - just simply the practice of knowing where your center is and coming back into it.

Right now, we want to help you find that.

Again, take a deep, deep deep breath.

Imagine the rod of energy we mentioned before that goes all the way up and down your spine and that reaches all the way through the cosmos into Source and back again, through the center of earth and back up into the base of your spine. You can access an entire mediation just on experiencing this flow at **www.livingtheonelight.com.**

But for now, come to that thick, beautiful, resonant pole of energy running up and down your spine and through the entire cosmos, all the way back around and down and up through the core of earth and back into the base of your spine.

Feel that rope, that rod running through your spinal column.

And now take a deep breath and feel and see and notice where your energy seems to be centered. For many people, it will be out in front of their hearts, running ahead to get the next thing done. For others, it may be up above your heads, scared and trying to escape something. For others, maybe it is happily settled deep in your pelvis or your womb holding that golden light of energy and allowing it to circulate. For others, maybe it is centered in your heart allowing feelings to move or hoping to help stuck feelings to circulate out and to flow.

Wherever your energy seems to be centered in this movement, take a deep, deep, deep breath and connect to your energy center just as it is, right here and right now.

Now bring your attention and your awareness to that energy center and gently imagine the arms and hands of your heart and your highest being and your highest knowing to gently grasp your energy center and bring it back into your body, in through your heart, and through the back of your heart center, back until it touches and clicks with your beautiful, glowing orb of the cord of light going up and down your spine and through all of existence.

Take a deep, deep breath and feel your essence, your center of your energy to sit, to click, to be back where it belongs - in the center of your being, back into your pelvis and in the cord of your spinal column, at the base of your heart.

And sit with your self centered in these two places and just breathe.... and know.....

And ebb and flow and fill and release.

And in this place, perhaps put one hand on your pelvis and one hand on your heart and feel and know anything and everything you can let go of and anything and everything you need to rejuvenate, to replenish your golden glow.

And allow all that needs to go to go and all that needs to enter to refill and replenish you in your healing, golden glow.

And in this deep, still knowing, rest, receive, and sleep and sleep and sleep and be....

CLEARING

Ok, so, dear friends...

I have given you some suggestions of what steps to take if you feel called to open your cells, open your selves to remembering all of who you are, all of why you and I are here, and what we have come to do.

The next crucial step in this process, as you are opening is also that you are clearing.

Clearing, letting go, releasing, over and over and over again, until you rebecome the clear channel of love and high vibrational energy that you are.

This clearing, this letting go is crucial as well, and it can be and needs to be done as you are ready and on so many levels, we can not even conceive of all of these levels and layers and ways that the clearing needs to and will happen.

Remember, you are a cosmic, multidimensional, high level being.

Also remember that this means that you simultaneously co-exist in many frequencies and in many dimensions all at the same time, all at once.

This means that as you are transmuting, letting go, and releasing things, you are doing so for all of existence. You might at first have stories about what you are releasing or why and this is fine.

Allow the stories to flow.

Stories are holograms, are portals, are mirrors for many existences.

Stories allow energies to rise and fall, for tears to come, for laughter to happen.

Stories give a structure and a sense of "why" that many times the human mind needs to feel safe in remembering and allowing to transmute energies that are flowing.

At first, most often, you will allow to flow and let go of stories in your immediate past or present life. You will have very concrete stories attached to these energies that you are letting to flow.

Then you will maybe begin to remember and release and let go of energies that feel like they are attached to what you might experience as "past lives" on the Earthly plane.

And as you release these, you will perhaps begin to realize that you are also accessing other dimensions, other timelines, other entities that are you, other beings that are part of your storying, your telling of the movements of lives throughout all of existence.

Over time and through these experiences of letting go, you will realize that you are actually transmitting and letting go of energies that are not only related to stories linked to you, you are releasing and letting go of energies and motions of things that are of all of existence, all lifetimes, all beings, all frequencies of all that is.

That is you.

That is us.

We are truly all one.

And so we are transmuting, healing, releasing from our bodies and from ourselves the energies that need to move out of us, through us, through all of time and space and through existence beyond time and space.

And this is beautiful, this is amazing.

This is deep, deep, incredible, ultimate healing.

And when we release all of the energies that need to move, that need to release from and through us, we suddenly are free!

This ultimate, cosmic dance of freedom is not about being free from suffering, free from control of another human, free in the senses of the word that we often associate with it.

This version of ultimate, highest freedom means that finally, and again, we are in our highest, ultimate version of ourselves! We are released back into our natural state that is needed ultimately by all of existence - we are back in our states as free, separate, and amazingly connected transmitters of pure light and highest, most pure love, and all of the

highest, most pure vibrational frequencies that need to move throughout the universes and throughout all of time and space and beyond in all of existence.

This is the ultimate freedom.

This is the ultimate dance.

And this is what we came here to do.

Thank you....

FLOWING: REMEMBERING YOUR SONG, YOUR MEDICINE, AND CO-CREATION WITH ME

So what is the point of all of this?

Why would you want to release into this reality that I, Gaia, the goddess mama of your Earth, and all of you are ultimately transmitters of the highest of all frequencies in all of existence?

As I have mentioned, the ultimate reason and need for this is far beyond most of human comprehension at this moment.

So part of the answer from us is, "Just trust us."

However, some of it can be put into human consciousness and human words at this time.

First of all, being a transmitter of ultimate, highest love, light, and beyond is ecstatic, it is beautiful flow. It is a reminder for you of all that is, of why you are here, and gives you a sense of centering and grounding and purpose.

Second, it is an invitation to remember so much more. Much of the purpose of being this transmitter of highest vibrational energies is that you then become a transmitter and a see-er and a knower of the highest, most deep, most pure, most timeless knowings of all that is. One way to put it is - you remember your own and the cosmic songs.

You have gifts and talents and deep knowledge, some of which you realize, and some of which you don't, that needs to come through specifically you.

It is akin to each person or animal plant or life force being a truly unique pair of filter glasses. Energy is energy and a frequency is a frequency. However, your selves, your souls, the structures of your energy bodies and your physical bodies are beautiful, crystalline structures and exquisite, healing filters for these energies and frequencies. And every single one of you is exquisitely unique, just like every single snow flake or or every single flower petal is perfect and singly its own being, every single time. The form of energy that needs to exquisitely and beautifully come through exactly YOU can ONLY come through EXACTLY YOU!

The song that is YOU can only come through you. The songs of the cosmos that need to come through you are sung as you sing them ONLY by you!

And so how can this happen?

There is only ONE WAY.

This has to happen by you allowing the intricate, gorgeous details of your exact, perfect form to open, to shine, to clear any and all dust or gunk, to let go and let go and let go until the incredible gem that is exactly you is fully open, and fully flowing with all of the light of all of cosmic life force that needs to move through you in each moment.

This happens when the gem that is you is shining open and wide, singing its exact, perfect song, just exactly as it was meant to from its first inception.

Just imagine us each and all as our full, whole, open, completely alive, shining, resonant, singing selves lighting up the sky, bursting wide all over this Earth and throughout the cosmos, in harmony , in rhythm, in time with each other.

This is a miracle, but a possible one.

Remember, I am a gem and a song too.

And my song directly is singing to and through you all the time.

So imagine this –

I am opening, I am filling with all of life force of all of the stars, of all of the light beams, of all of all of existence, in tandem with our sun, with all of our friends, the planets, every single galaxy, every single one of the swirling, twirling, ever expanding and moving and growing universes in all of existence.

And as I am opening and filling with my entire, full life force, and as I am breathing in all that I am and all that is, and as I am releasing and allowing to move through me all that is moving and transmuting and letting go through me, so are you!

Do you feel this too?

I am moving with you.

I am moving through you.

My life force is filled with the cosmos, as are you, and as you open, you are filled with me.

Our songs are coming forward through our beings, through all of who we are and we are resonating in frequency, in pitch, in highest, most resonant, most beautiful of ringing that rises and falls with the cadence, the rhythm, the exquisite voices and calls and touches and reaches of every single thing that exists in all of everywhere.

We can know and we can see and we can be and we can hear and we can remember literally ALL THAT IS.

And that is why we are here!

Together.

Do you remember, my dear, old, very special and incredibly beautiful friend?

This is why we are here.

Take my hands?

Kneel down with me.

Look straight into my eyes.

Feel me going straight into your soul and you going straight into my soul.

I love you.

More than time and space and all of existence can possibly imagine.

I love you through and through and through and through.

We are beauty.

We are love.

We are highest love beyond what most people on this planet can fathom, but we will remember.

We are so incredible.

And we are knowing.

Rest in this knowing.

Rest in and on me.

I am here.

I am holding you.

I am your mother while you are on my body.

Let me love you.

Let me know you and hold you and love you completely, through and through.

You are safe.

You are perfect.

You are here.

You are held.

You are the stars.

Every single one.

And we are one.

Open the gem of all of who you are.

Feel the power and the vibration of the songs that are truly you.

Feel the songs coming through your heart, through your chest, through all of who you are.

Feel your song reach out into space, into all of everything that exists.

And feel the songs of infinite beings reaching your songs.

And let the songs mix.

Feel the harmonies moving through you.

Feel the harmonics, the rhythms, the healing, the exquisiteness of knowing all that is.

Feel the beautiful medicine of your song and of all the songs of existence.

Feel the incredible gratitude of existence that you are here.

THANK YOU.

SO MUCH LOVE....

GAIA SPEAKS VISUALIZATIONS
YOU ARE A GODDESS, YOU ARE A GOD:

I want you to remember this.

I am looking you straight in the eyes. I have my hands on your hips and I am reminding you. Feel your body, feel your strength, feel your beauty that transcends literally everything. You are rainbows, you are stardust, you are aliveness bursting into flames, you are incredible.

And so know this... remember this. And relax... so deeply relax.

It is all ok.

In this knowing, you can remember that you are perfect. You are safe. You can not only relax physically, you can also relax energetically.

In this knowing, you can allow all of your whole being to come fully present into your body, you can allow all of you to fill every cavity of your body, every part of your cells.

Take another deep breath and do this over and over and over again.

Notice that there might be parts of your body filling back up.

Notice that there might be rivers of your self and your spirit and your knowing and your being that are coming back on line. There might be pockets of empty space or cringing or fear that are relaxing, that are filling, that are suddenly smiling, that are allowing and remembering that you love them.

This is so beautiful.

This is it.

Remember that you are actually exquisite love.

Take a deep, deep, deep breath.

And I am crying again as I watch you remembering this and allowing your body to remember this - you ARE love.

Every part of you is love.

Any word or deed that might have occurred in this lifetime or in other lifetimes or existences on or off this planet that have been anything other than love are not real.

You ARE love.

Repeat this.

Let this reverberate in you.

You ARE love.

Love is filling you now.

Love is all that you are.

Let go, let love completely fill you, fill you back up, remember this knowing.

Gods, goddesses, exquisite creatures of the cosmos, you ARE beings of pure love.

It is so.

DIVINE SEXUALITY VISUALIZATION:

First, I want you to take a deep, deep, deep breath.

I want you to remember who you are - you come from me, I come from the cosmos - literally. So you are the stars. You are from the same physical and energetic material that made the stars. Literally. You are AMAZING. Breathe that in....

You are amazing.....

You are made from all of existence....

Literally....

And so, here on this planet, here in your body, right now, take another deep breath.

And feel my energy rising.

Feel a warm, powerful feeling of light and life and love rising up the inside of your feet into the insides of your calves, up the insides of your thighs, and into your pelvic area. Feel this energy circulating inside of your pelvis, inside of your womb or your abdomen. Feel this energy circulating into a tiny ball of glowing, happy, healing, golden light.

In the center of this place, you will notice and feel a warm, knowing place. This is the center of a place of your being and a place where you can rest. Here, it is safe.

Take another deep breath.

Feel into this place that is warm and know that you are safe here.

Imagine that that warmth is a light (it is!). And imagine that the light is pulsing with life (because again, it is!). And imagine that light is like a little ball, maybe the size of a small pom pom ball.

If you want to stay fairly grounded and centered, this may be how you choose to complete this experience. Or you may follow your own wisdom in the moment and allow your consciousness and your life essence presence to take you on journeys that only you may know.

As you follow this experience over and over again, you will learn to know yourself again in a way that you might not yet be able to fathom.

And as you do this, your healing, loving light will open you and take you to places and parts of your own wisdom and your own life that you might not have even realized you were meant to live.

This is beautiful.

You are beautiful.

You are literally life itself.

You are wise.

You are love.

You are loved.

You so deeply love.

You so deeply love yourself.

The stars hold you.

All of life is in you.

All of life is in love with you. Literally.

You and the stars are made of the same essence and the same spark.

Every single one of your cells holds your life essence and your love and your deepest, ultimate wisdom and every single thing that you need.

You are exactly where you need to be.

You are exactly who you need to be.

Thank you for listening.

Thank you for being here.

Thank you for being you...

DEEP RESTING VISUALIZATION:

Again, take a deep, deep deep breath.

Imagine the rod of energy we mentioned before that goes all the way up and down your spine and that reaches all the way through the cosmos into Source and back again, through the center of Earth and back up into the base of your spine. You can access an entire mediation on experiencing this flow at **www.livingtheonelight.com.**

But for now, come to that thick, beautiful, resonant pole of energy running up and down your spine and through the entire cosmos, all the way back around and down and up through the core of earth and back into the base of your spine.

Feel that rope, that rod running through your spinal column.

And now take a deep breath and feel and see and notice where your energy seems to be centered. For many people, it will be out in front of their hearts, running ahead to get the next thing done. For others, it may be up above your heads, scared and trying to escape something. For others, maybe it is happily settled deep in your pelvis or your womb holding that golden light of energy and allowing it to circulate. For others, maybe it is centered in your heart allowing feelings to move or hoping to help stuck feelings to circulate out and to flow.

Wherever your energy seems to be centered in this movement, take a deep, deep, deep breath and connect to your energy center just as it is, right here and right now.

Now bring your attention and your awareness to that energy center and gently imagine the arms and hands of your heart and your highest being and your highest knowing to gently grasp your energy center and bring it back into your body, in through your heart, and through the back of your heart center, back until it touches and clicks with your beautiful, glowing orb of the cord of light going up and down your spine and through all of existence.

Take a deep, deep breath and feel your essence, your center of your energy to sit, to click, to be back where it belongs - in the center of your being, back into your pelvis and in the cord of your spinal column, at the base of your heart.

And sit with your self centered in these two places and just breathe.... and know.....

And ebb and flow and fill and release.

And in this place, perhaps put one hand on your pelvis and one hand on your heart and feel and know anything and everything you can let go of and anything and everything you need to rejuvenate, to replenish your golden glow.

And allow all that needs to go to go and all that needs to enter to refill and replenish you in your healing, golden glow.

And in this deep, still knowing, rest, receive, and sleep and sleep and sleep and be....

YOUR BEAUTIFUL WISDOM - JOURNALING PAGES

In these pages, allow whatever needs to come through you to come through. You can fill these pages with words or images or songs or anything else that comes through the beautiful being that is you as you go through this book and through these visualizations or at any other time in your day. Follow the prompts on each page or create your own way of allowing your beautiful wisdom to flow.

So much love...

My Love Letter to Gaia... My Dedication to You...

I am a Goddess, I am a God...

Hello, Sun, My Friend and Mentor...

I Dance, I Sing, I Move...

Love Flows Through Me...

I Breathe and Resonate with All I Imbibe...

I Come to Center and Deeply Rest and Reset...

I Release and Release and Release and Am Clear...

I am a Star, I am a Song, I am a Medicine.

I Remember. I Flow...

ABOUT MARTHA

Martha Alter Hines, MSW, CMT is a channel and a cosmic healer. She has twenty years of experience in the very grounded world as a psychotherapist, clinical social worker, and body worker.

She now assists people to navigate the beautiful and often challenging experience of awakening to their ultimate, cosmic selves and souls. She has the grounded experience as a psychotherapist and body worker, but also has many spiritual gifts which include the ability to see people's actual souls, their energy bodies, past lives, spiritual worlds, and the energy bodies and structures of the Earth and of the cosmos. Martha, therefore, has an ability to bridge both the Earthly world and that of the spiritual and cosmic worlds and to help people to navigate this balance.

Martha is in constant communication with a wide range of spiritual energies and existences and is channeling a series of books that are voices of many of these entities. Each book is a different medicine to also assist people in their awakening journeys. The first book, Living the One Light, was published in 2018. Gaia Speaks is the second book in the series and many more are yet to come.

Martha has two beautiful children and lives in gorgeous Goleta, California. Martha loves the coast of California and feels called to be co-creating with this place for a long time to come.

*Connect with Martha for mentoring and cosmic healing work at **www.livingtheonelight.com** and **livingtheonelight@gmail.com***